Contents

Harvests and happiness

WITH GONGS AND DANCING, flowers and firecrackers, the Chinese New Year warms the cold winter. The New Year is also known as the Spring Festival, bringing hopes for a good harvest in the year to come.

WHO CELEBRATES?

Throughout most of China, Taiwan and Hong Kong, Chinese New Year explodes in city streets and in the countryside. Chinese people living in other parts of the world also celebrate the New Year with flowers and firecrackers and special food.

Chinese New Year's Day is a public holiday for the whole country. Many people carry on celebrating for several days.

TIME TO CELEBRATE

Chinese New Year starts somewhere between late January and the middle of February. The date changes from year to year because it follows an ancient farming calendar.

New Year calendars are on sale in the Chinese part of London. Red is a lucky colour for the Chinese.

In southern China, bundles of grain are being turned so that they dry off properly. During the Spring Festival the farmer will be hoping that the next year's crop is just as good as this one.

A lion dancer is going to do battle with another lion – or maybe a cockerel. Sometimes there are monkey dancers – and clowns, too. Lion dances take place in Chinese communities throughout the world, from California to Calcutta.

Animal antics

EVERY NEW YEAR IN CHINA is named after one of twelve animals, each animal taking it in turn. The year 2,000 will be the Year of the Dragon! Animal signs are used for festivals and religious ceremonies, birthdays and working out horoscopes. Look at the birth-year animals. Which one are you?

If you start with Rat and move to the right you will follow the cycle of years. To find out which animals are which look on page 9.

AN ANIMAL ARGUMENT! How did the animals decide which of them should start the cycle of years? Here is just one of the stories.

The animals were having an argument. Each of them wanted to be the very first Animal of the Year. So the gods said that the animals must have a race across a river. The winner would start the cycle of years.

All the animals leapt into the water together. But the strong Ox soon took the lead. The other animals struggled on behind - all except Rat. No one had noticed him crouched on Ox's back. Just before Ox touched the other side, Rat leapt on to the bank and won the race!

Rat 1972, 1984, 1996 You have a hot temper, but a lot of charm. You always finish what you set out to do.

Ox 1973, 1985, 1997 You are quiet, calm and can keep a secret. You like doing things on your own.

Tiger 1974, 1986, 1998 You are brave and have a strong will. You are loving, but can get a bit angry.

Rabbit 1975, 1987, 1999 You are lucky, but deserve it because you are patient and not greedy. You are shy and a bit moody sometimes.

Dragon 1976, 1988, 2000 You like to be the leader - you talk a lot and sometimes ask a bit too much of other people. You can be sensitive.

Snake 1977, 1989, 2001 You are wise and attractive, but sometimes you boast. You can also be a bit mean.

Horse 1978, 1990, 2002 You are independent, clever and people admire you. You are cheerful and like talking!

Ram 1979, 1991, 2003 You are artistic, calm and caring. You also know how to use your talents well. But you can't always make up your mind!

Monkey 1980, 1992, 2004 You have a lot of good in you. You are creative and successful but can be troublesome!

Rooster 1981, 1993, 2005 You are clever and hardworking. Sometimes you like to be alone, dreaming of great things. You are usually modest– but not always.

Dog 1982, 1994, 2006 You are very hardworking and loyal. Justice is important to you. But you have rather a strong will.

Pig 1983, 1995, 2007 You have a strong character - in a quiet sort of way. You like to learn - but only about the things that interest you.

Rites and rituals

FOR MANY PEOPLE, Chinese New Year is a religious festival as well as a lot of fun. It began long ago when there was only one religion which had many gods and spirits. Nowadays, New Year is also celebrated in the temples of newer faiths.

GODS THAT GUARD YOU

The ancient Chinese religion had many Door Gods in the house to watch over the family. One story about a Door God guard takes us back a thousand years.

Emperor Taizong had fallen ill, and one night he lay tossing and turning in his bed. He had a really bad dream. Ghosts howled and screamed in his head all night. The next day he told his two best soldiers, Qin Qiong and Yuchi Gong, about the dream.

The next night, these good soldiers stood outside the emperor's bedroom door. One held a club and the other, an iron rod. In the morning, the emperor said that he had slept like a log. But the soldiers could not

At this Buddhist temple, people will light joss sticks and say prayers for a peaceful New Year.

▶ This Door God guard was once a famous soldier. Every New Year people put up his picture to guard their homes.

spend every night guarding his room. So the emperor told an artist to paint pictures of the two soldiers. These were hung as guards on the palace gates.

Word soon got round that the paintings were guarding the palace against evil spirits. People started to stick pictures of the two soldiers outside their homes, too. Nowadays, at New Year, millions of Door God pictures flutter in the winter wind.

~A festival diary~

FIND OUT WHAT HAPPENS at Chinese New Year by following this festive diary! Long ago, the fun lasted for 15 days. But now, most people only celebrate the first three days of the festival.

BE PREPARED!

There's plenty of work to be done before the New Year fun begins. First, everyone helps to clean the house from top to toe. Lots of food is prepared for New Year's Day. Lucky red decorations are hung over doors and around rooms. Flower fairs and gift stalls are set up. All debts have to paid back, too. This is not so important as it used to be. Long ago, people had to hide if they owed money to someone!

Flowers are a symbol of plenty at New Year. There are lots to choose from here!

The doors are sealed – nothing bad can get in now, and the good luck stays inside.

NEW YEAR'S EVE

Not many people go to bed on New Year's Eve. The streets buzz with happy people, young and old alike. Temples are full of worshippers. Families gather from far and wide to eat a special meal together.

Some families still follow the old New Year traditions. They stay in the house and shut the doors and windows tight to stop evil spirits getting in. Tree branches are burned and firecrackers set off to drive the spirits away. On New Year's morning the doors and windows are unlocked and good wishes are spoken. Now the New Year celebrations can really begin!

A wedding procession at New Year in a village in northern China

On New Year's Day, you can ...

shout 'Happy New Year! and hope for wealth for everyone. Children hope to get little red parcels with 'lucky money' inside them! Families gather together - everyone wearing their new clothes. At the crowded dinner table, you won't see much meat. Many people do not eat meat on New Year's Day.

But on New Year's Day you can't...

wash! At least, people didn't in days gone by. They did take a long bath on New Year's Eve, though. You mustn't clean the house, either. If you do, all the wealth that the gods have brought for the new year will be swept away. Try not to break anything as this will bring bad luck. So will falling over or using bad language. And don't use any knives or scissors, will you?

On the second day...

People visit family and friends. Some go gambling. New Year is the only time when gambling is not frowned upon.

On the third day...

Don't go visiting people - it's bound to end up in an argument! But you could visit a temple and find out your future with fortune sticks.

These Chinese dolls are a very special decoration. They're holding New Year money packets with clasped hands. The hands show that they greet people with good wishes for the future.

Red and gold are lucky colours used on these money packets.

14

On the fourth day...

Nowadays most people start returning to normal. But teams of dancers dress up and dance in the streets (see page 20).

From the fifth to the fifteenth day...

You can clean the house and get back to work now, or go to the sales to look for bargains. All the gods in Heaven gather together on the eighth day. Some people ask for their blessings. And on the ninth day, you could burn some incense for the birthday of the Jade Emperor, the king of the gods. Finally, between the tenth and the fifteenth days, you can buy lanterns with good wishes written on them. The Lantern Festival ends the New Year celebrations. Find out more about it on page 28!

People in Hong Kong are choosing fortune sticks to take to the temple. The way the sticks fall shows the kind of luck the person will have.

Fire and light

MILLIONS OF FIRECRACKERS explode and sparkle on New Year's Day. Today they are mostly just for fun. Long ago, they were set off to keep away evil spirits in the year to come.

GHOSTS, MONSTERS AND EVIL SPIRITS

Nowadays, firecrackers bring joy and laughter. But in ancient times, it was believed that the noise and bright lights of the firecrackers chased away ghosts and devils, too. They also frightened off a huge mountain giant. At the end of the old year, this angry beast came down from the mountain to kill every living creature in sight. But people noticed that it was scared of flashes of light and loud bangs. So bamboo stems were set alight to make the monster run straight back up the mountain.

THE FIRST FIRECRACKERS

In ancient times, people set fire to bamboo stems. The stems are hollow inside except for joints along their length. When the bamboo is lit, the air inside the stems expands. The pressure is so great, the bamboo suddenly splits open with a loud crack! Nowadays, firecrackers are made with cardboard and chemicals.

QUIET LIGHT

Many people visit temples during the Spring Festival to pray for peace and success. They also light hundreds of joss sticks for good luck. The word 'joss' was brought to China by early Portuguese explorers. It was actually 'Deos', which means 'God'. Joss sticks are made of thin strips of bamboo cane dipped in sawdust and sweet-smelling powder made from tree gums.

Firework displays light up
the harbour in Hong
Kong during New Year.

People light joss sticks in a
Chinese temple in Malaysia.

Peachwood and poems

IN ANCIENT TIMES, charms made of peachwood were lucky symbols. Rhymes of good fortune were written on them. Nowadays, these rhymes are printed on strips of red paper. They are stuck on doors all over the house.

IMPORTANT PEACHES

Over a thousand years ago, New Year messages were written on small peachwood charms. They were hung on gates to protect the home. Later, these short messages were written as two-line poems, called Spring couplets.

RHYMES ON RED PAPER

Nowadays, the couplets are printed on red paper. They are stuck around the home, especially on doors. Here are some of the verses of hope for the future:

Peaceful days throughout the years
Spring of good luck forever

May your happiness be as wide as the East Sea

May you have a favourable wind all the way

The Chinese writing for 'peach' also means long life - so peaches are thought to be lucky. So at New Year, people buy a small peach tree, or some peach blossom.

▶ No wonder this woman is smiling! Her doorway is surrounded by hopeful messages on red paper. People wish for peace, wealth, a long life, many children and even power.

Drums and dancing

GONGS, DRUMS AND CYMBALS ring and crash throughout New Year, especially in southern China. Dancers in animal and clown costumes mime and somersault or walk on stilts.

DEAFENING DRUMS!

In the south of China, villages take part in the New Year drum competitions. Each band has a drum, a pair of cymbals and a few gongs. A team plays to the rhythm of its own drum, but all the bands perform at the same time. The music thunders like cannons as each band tries to overpower all the others!

DANCING LIONS

Between the fourth and the fifteenth days of the New Year, teams of dancers tour the countryside. Each team has about ten dancers, all dressed in the same trousers, jackets and hats. They are armed with swords and clubs, rather like soldiers. But among these dancers come bright paper heads of lions, cats and roosters, decorated with ringing bells.

Dancers hold the heads and move them to the sound of drums and

Up in the mountains in Qinghai province, expert stilt dancers parade down the street in bright costumes.

gongs. Their bodies leap in the air or roll on the ground just like the beasts they are meant to be. Dancers in monkey and clown costumes twist, somersault and joke in front of the crowd.

A New Year dragon
dance in New York

This rooster will face a lion during a New Year lion dance

21

Festive food

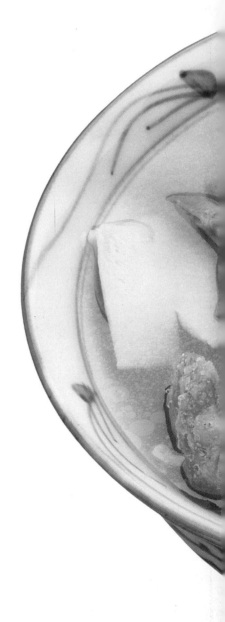

HEAPS OF STICKY CAKES and plump dumplings are eaten over the Spring Festival! The vast farming areas of China produce an enormous variety of foods. These are made into favourite dishes at this time of year.

PREPARING FOR A PARTY

It takes a long time to prepare food for the long New Year festivities. In the south, heaps of rice grains are sorted and washed several days before the celebrations. This way, the job will be done in good time. The huge mounds of rice are also a symbol of hope for a good harvest next year.

Dates, chestnuts, walnuts, hazelnuts, melon seeds, lotus seeds and oranges are favourite snacks. The word used for each often sounds like a word meaning something lucky.

Duck, chicken and goose are favourite festive meats. But people do not just tuck in greedily. Meat and fish are also taken to shrines and offered to the gods and spirits.

SWEET SUCCESS

On New Year's Eve and New Year's Day in northern China, sweet dumplings are shaped like the golden shoes that were used as money in ancient China. If you are extra lucky, you could find a coin in your dumpling!

In southern China, it is thought to be very lucky to eat lots of sticky cakes.

Fruit is very popular at New Year – especially mandarins.

Many people tuck into Won Ton soup at New Year.

Faraway festivities

CHINESE NEW YEAR is not only celebrated in China! In other parts of southeast Asia and in cities from America to Britain, Chinese communities put on their biggest festival.

A SCATTERED PEOPLE

Chinese people have been leaving China's mainland for hundreds of years. Most went to other parts of southeast Asia, such as Vietnam, Hong Kong and Malaysia.

About 150 years ago, some Chinese left for America, Canada and Australia. Here, they worked on the railways or in gold mines.

Chinese communities can also be found in other countries such as Britain. The city areas where they live are called Chinatown. Here, many Chinese people still keep to their traditional ways.

People are buying decorations for New Year in London's Chinatown.

Dazzling lights in Singapore show that New Year has arrived!

CHINESE NEW YEAR FAR AWAY

In New York's Chinatown, New Year brings dragon dancers and exploding firecrackers to the streets. There are about 400 Chinese restaurants in this small area. At this time of year they offer grand feasts.

Do you like being scared? If so, you can follow the 25-metre long fierce dragon in San Francisco's Golden Dragon Parade. In Malaysia, on the fifteenth day of the festival, women throw an orange into the sea. It is supposed to help them find a good husband. Chinese opera, with singing, cymbals and gongs is performed free on the streets.

In Hong Kong, the children chant a special New Year rhyme wishing for lots of money wrapped up in lucky red parcels. But the rhyme also wishes for happiness for everyone. This is the true spirit of Chinese New Year wherever it is celebrated.

25

Lighting lanterns

THE LANTERN FESTIVAL is a bright and happy way to end the long celebrations. It takes place under the light of the New Year's first full moon.

THE LANTERN FESTIVAL LONG AGO

More than 2,000 years ago, people swung lanterns under the full moon on the fifteenth day of the New Year. Spring was getting closer - days were longer and the

▶ This lantern in lucky red and gold has a prayer of hope written on it.

This is how a lantern shop looked more than 150 years ago.

sun a little stronger. So the celebration took place in honour of the Sun God, then known as the Lord of the East.

About 500 years later, the festival also marked the day when a cruel ruler was driven from power. The wise and kind Emperor Wen had taken over. Every year, on the night of the Lantern Festival, he went out on to the streets to celebrate the freedom of his people.

DECORATIONS AND DANCING

Nowadays, city streets, homes, restaurants, shops and market places glow with coloured lights. In villages, lanterns are tied to strings and then hung in a tent-shape from a strong pole. Animal lanterns, especially dragons, are carried along the streets in long processions. Families gather to watch masked dancers parading around the towns and villages.

Lantern-frames are made of bamboo, wood, iron, wheat stalks or even animal horn. They are covered with thin coloured paper, silk, glass or plastic. In the cold northeast, lights are shone through shapes carved from ice. But perhaps the most beautiful are the colourful paper figures that spin round the bright light of a candle.

A paper-lantern market is crammed with lucky red and gold lanterns.

27

~ Let's celebrate! ~

Join in the fun! Try making this lion mask and lucky red packet. You can get lots of ideas by looking at the pictures of lion masks and lucky packets in the book.

MAKING A LION MASK

All you need are:
1. a large open cardboard box
2. some poster paints and a brush
3. sticky tape and PVA glue
4. safe scissors
5. materials to decorate your lion; you could paint strips of newspaper or you could use silver foil, wool, ribbon, tissue paper, crêpe paper, sequins... anything goes!

All you have to do is:
1. Paint your box in bright colours.
2. Cut holes in the box for the lion's mouth and eyes (ask an adult to help with this).
3. Stick on the lion's tongue, mane and beard with sticky tape.
4. Use PVA glue for sequins and other decorations.

MAKING A LUCKY RED PACKET

All you need are:
1 a piece of paper
2 red and yellow paint and a brush
3 safe scissors
4 PVA glue

Your lucky red packet will look like this.

All you have to do is:
1 Cut out your paper in the shape shown in the diagram.
2 Paint your paper red on one side.
3 Fold the side flaps in along the dotted lines in the diagram.
4 Fold up the bottom half of the paper along the dotted line.
5 Glue the flaps to the inside of the bottom half.
6 Stick a yellow lucky shape on your packet. Fat, leaping fish, plump grain and bouncing babies are all lucky!

Glossary

blessings wishes of joy and happiness

celebrate to show that a certain day or event is special

celebration ways of showing that a day or event is special, such as parades or parties

ceremonies ways of celebrating a special event or day – sometimes they are more solemn and serious than a celebration

communities groups of people who live and work together

horoscope a description of a person's future and character using, for example, their birth date and the position of the stars

procession a long line of people walking or dancing along a street

spirits beings that you can't see – a bit like ghosts

traditional describes very old ways of living that parents teach to their children

worshippers people who show respect to gods and spirits through prayers and songs

Index